To my Beautiful Daughter:

_____

Dear Daughter

I love you

Mom and Me

I love
you
So much

FRIENDS ARE
Everything

Best friend

YEARLY *Overview*

January
_____
_____
_____
_____
_____
_____
_____

February
_____
_____
_____
_____
_____
_____
_____

March
_____
_____
_____
_____
_____
_____
_____

April
_____
_____
_____
_____
_____
_____
_____

May
_____
_____
_____
_____
_____
_____
_____

June
_____
_____
_____
_____
_____
_____
_____

July
_____
_____
_____
_____
_____
_____
_____

August
_____
_____
_____
_____
_____
_____
_____

September
_____
_____
_____
_____
_____
_____
_____

October
_____
_____
_____
_____
_____
_____
_____

November
_____
_____
_____
_____
_____
_____
_____

December
_____
_____
_____
_____
_____
_____
_____

LOST IN **ADVENTURE**

BOOKS TO READ:

_____

_____

_____

_____

_____

_____

_____

_____

_____

_____

_____

_____

_____

_____

BOOK OF THE MONTH

READING GOALS

FAVORITE AUTHORS

CURRENTLY READING

enjoy your life

MOVIES
To Watch

MOVIE TITLE:	RATING:
_____	☆☆☆☆☆ ▢
_____	☆☆☆☆☆ ▢
_____	☆☆☆☆☆ ▢
_____	☆☆☆☆☆ ▢
_____	☆☆☆☆☆ ▢
_____	☆☆☆☆☆ ▢
_____	☆☆☆☆☆ ▢
_____	☆☆☆☆☆ ▢
_____	☆☆☆☆☆ ▢
_____	☆☆☆☆☆ ▢
_____	☆☆☆☆☆ ▢
_____	☆☆☆☆☆ ▢
_____	☆☆☆☆☆ ▢
_____	☆☆☆☆☆ ▢
_____	☆☆☆☆☆ ▢
_____	☆☆☆☆☆ ▢
_____	☆☆☆☆☆ ▢
_____	☆☆☆☆☆ ▢
_____	☆☆☆☆☆ ▢

MOVIE *Tracker*

MOVIE TITLE:

- [ ] _____
- [ ] _____
- [ ] _____
- [ ] _____
- [ ] _____
- [ ] _____
- [ ] _____
- [ ] _____
- [ ] _____
- [ ] _____
- [ ] _____
- [ ] _____
- [ ] _____
- [ ] _____
- [ ] _____
- [ ] _____

MOVIE TITLE:

- [ ] _____
- [ ] _____
- [ ] _____
- [ ] _____
- [ ] _____
- [ ] _____
- [ ] _____
- [ ] _____
- [ ] _____
- [ ] _____
- [ ] _____
- [ ] _____
- [ ] _____
- [ ] _____
- [ ] _____
- [ ] _____

TRAVEL *Plans*

PLACES I WANT TO VISIT:

- ☐ _____
- ☐ _____
- ☐ _____
- ☐ _____
- ☐ _____
- ☐ _____
- ☐ _____
- ☐ _____
- ☐ _____
- ☐ _____
- ☐ _____
- ☐ _____
- ☐ _____

MY TOP 3 SPOTS:

MUST-SEE SIGHTS:

ATTRACTIONS:

go where you feel most alive

Television *Tracker*

TV SHOWS TO WATCH:

FAVORITE SERIES

FAVORITE CHANNELS

BINGE-WORTHY

HEALTHY *Living*

HEALTHY LIFE GOALS:

- [ ]
- [ ]
- [ ]
- [ ]
- [ ]
- [ ]

HEALTHY EATING GOALS:

- [ ]
- [ ]
- [ ]
- [ ]
- [ ]
- [ ]

BREAKFAST:

LUNCH:

DINNER:

Stay Strong

KEEPING IT
Real

WHAT'S MOST IMPORTANT TO ME:

_____

_____

_____

_____

_____

WHAT I'M MOST GRATEFUL FOR:

_____

_____

_____

_____

_____

♡ *smile* ♡

PERSONAL *Goals*

_____ _____
_____ _____
_____ _____
_____ _____
_____ _____
_____ _____
_____ _____
_____ _____
_____ _____
_____ _____
_____ _____
_____ _____

be wild ~ be true ~ be happy

THOUGHTS & REFLECTIONS

choose happy

DATES TO *Remember*

Daughter, live on the edge of adventure...

STAYING
On Track

TASKS & PROJECTS

☐
☐
☐
☐
☐
☐
☐
☐
☐
☐
☐

My Progress

MOM'S KITCHEN
To Mine

PREP TIME:

BAKE TIME:

Ingredients

Directions

STUFF I NEED *To Do*

DATE

GET STUFF DONE!

get stuff done

REMINDERS:

MY WEEK AHEAD

WHAT MY DAY LOOKS LIKE:

MONDAY

TUESDAY

WEDNESDAY

THURSDAY

REMINDERS & APPOINTMENTS:

MY WEEK AHEAD

WHAT MY DAY LOOKS LIKE:

FRIDAY

SATURDAY

SUNDAY

MY GREATEST ACCOMPISHMENTS THIS WEEK:

WEEKLY *Agenda*

monday

tuesday

wednesday

thursday

friday

saturday

sunday

GOAL: **DATE COMPLETED:**

NOTES & REMINDERS:

whatever
you are,
be a
good one

DATE

_____

PRIORITIES:

MY PERSONAL GOALS:

WHAT I HOPE TO ACCOMPLISH:

Good things take time

NOTES & REMINDERS:

live
MORE
worry
LeSS

Notes & Reminders

so there's a girl...
she stole my ♥ she calls me mom

love you to the moon and back...

DATE

DAILY TO DO LIST:

MY TOP PRIORITY OF THE DAY:

- [ ]
- [ ]
- [ ]
- [ ]
- [ ]
- [ ]
- [ ]
- [ ]
- [ ]
- [ ]
- [ ]
- [ ]
- [ ]
- [ ]
- [ ]
- [ ]

DON'T TELL PEOPLE YOUR Dreams SHOW THEM

Live
WHAT YOU
love

find your fire

the best
is yet
to come

shine
bright

Reminder from Mom

be·a·voice·
not·an·
echo

smile is the BEST make up

like mother, like daughter <3

you are
the star
in my sky

Notes & Stuff

-BE-

YOU

-tiful

believe

_____

_____

_____

_____

_____

_____

_____

_____

_____

_____

_____

_____

_____

_____

_____

_____

_____

THOUGHTS & REFLECTIONS

I'LL LOVE
YOU
forever
I'LL LIKE YOU
FOR
always
AS LONG
AS I'M LIVING
MY
Baby
YOU'LL
BE.

NOTES:

REMINDERS:

Daughter, live on the edge of adventure...

STAYING
On Track

TASKS & PROJECTS

My Progress

MOM'S KITCHEN
To Mine

PREP TIME:

BAKE TIME:

Ingredients

Directions

STUFF I NEED *To Do*

DATE

GET STUFF DONE!

get stuff Done

REMINDERS:

MY WEEK AHEAD

WHAT MY DAY LOOKS LIKE:

MONDAY

TUESDAY

WEDNESDAY

THURSDAY

REMINDERS & APPOINTMENTS:

MY WEEK AHEAD

WHAT MY DAY LOOKS LIKE:

FRIDAY

SATURDAY

SUNDAY

MY GREATEST ACCOMPISHMENTS THIS WEEK:

WEEKLY *Agenda*

monday

tuesday

wednesday

thursday

friday

saturday

sunday

GOAL:

DATE COMPLETED:

NOTES & REMINDERS:

Dream BIG

whatever
you are,
be a
good one

DATE

_____

PRIORITIES:

MY PERSONAL GOALS:

WHAT I HOPE TO ACCOMPLISH:

Good things take time

NOTES & REMINDERS:

live
MORE
worry
LESS

She
believed
SHE COULD
so she
did

_____
_____
_____
_____
_____
_____
_____
_____
_____
_____
_____
_____
_____
_____
_____
_____
_____
_____
_____
_____
_____

Notes & Reminders

so there's a girl...
she stole my ♥ she calls me mom

love you to the moon and back...

Daughter, live on the edge of adventure...

STAYING
On Track

TASKS & PROJECTS

☐
☐
☐
☐
☐
☐
☐
☐
☐
☐
☐
☐

My Progress

MOM'S KITCHEN
To Mine

PREP TIME:

BAKE TIME:

Ingredients

Directions

STUFF I NEED *To Do*

DATE

GET STUFF DONE!

REMINDERS:

MY WEEK AHEAD

WHAT MY DAY LOOKS LIKE:

MONDAY

TUESDAY

WEDNESDAY

THURSDAY

REMINDERS & APPOINTMENTS:

MY WEEK AHEAD

WHAT MY DAY LOOKS LIKE:

FRIDAY

SATURDAY

SUNDAY

MY GREATEST ACCOMPISHMENTS THIS WEEK:

WEEKLY *Agenda*

monday

tuesday

wednesday

thursday

friday

saturday

sunday

GOAL: **DATE COMPLETED:**

NOTES & REMINDERS:

whatever
you are.
be a
good one

Made in the USA
Coppell, TX
16 April 2020

20351563R00056